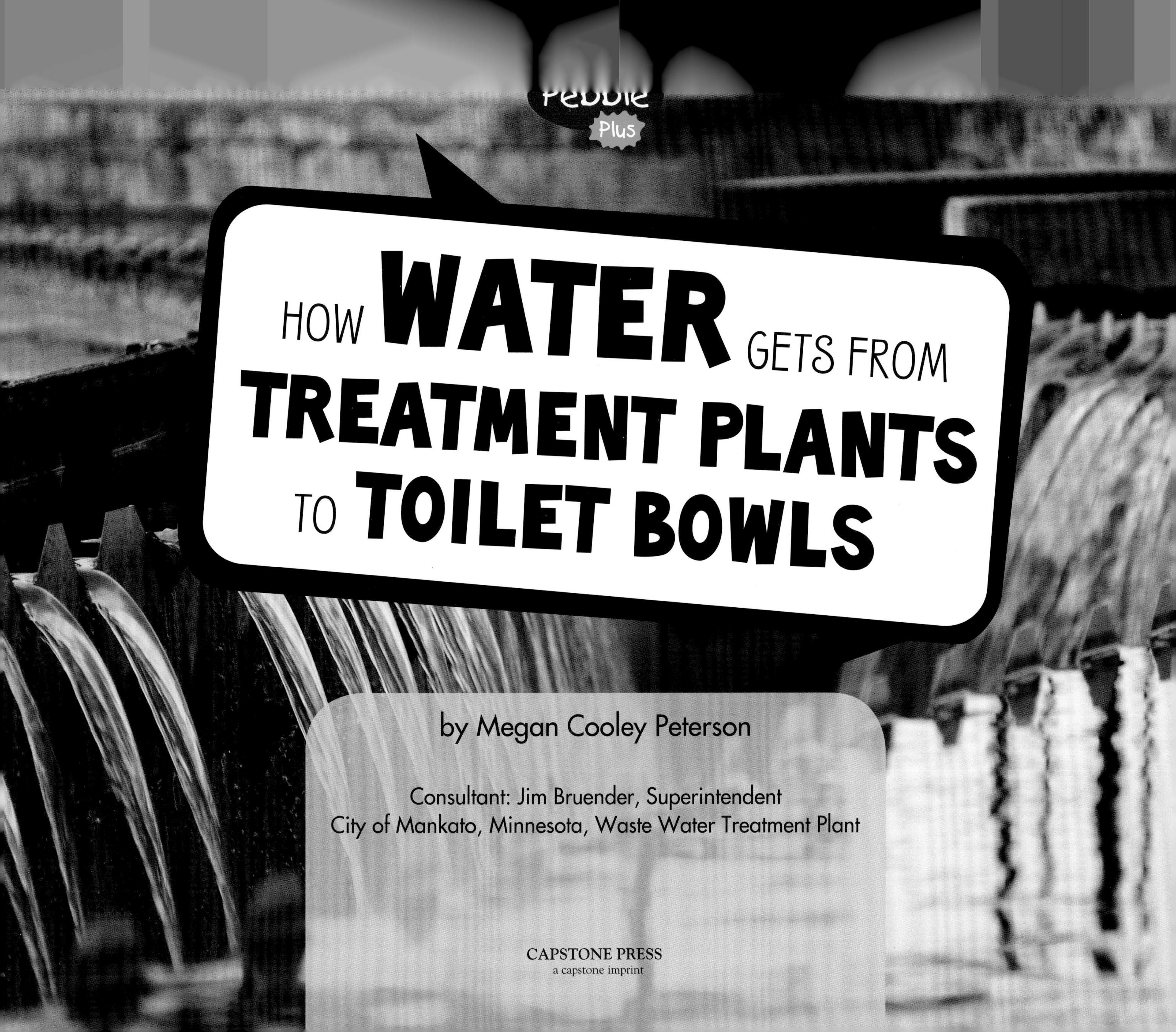

Pebble
Plus

HOW **WATER** GETS FROM **TREATMENT PLANTS** TO **TOILET BOWLS**

by Megan Cooley Peterson

Consultant: Jim Bruender, Superintendent
City of Mankato, Minnesota, Waste Water Treatment Plant

CAPSTONE PRESS
a capstone imprint

Pebble Plus is published by Capstone Press,
1710 Roe Crest Drive, North Mankato, Minnesota 56003
www.mycapstone.com

Library of Congress Cataloging-in-Publication Data
Cataloging-in-publication information is on file with the Library of Congress.
ISBN 978-1-4914-8435-7 (library binding)
ISBN 978-1-4914-8439-5 (paperback)
ISBN 978-1-4914-8443-2 (eBook PDF)

Editorial Credits
Jill Kalz, editor; Juliette Peters and Katelin Plekkenpol, designers;
Morgan Walters, media researcher; Laura Manthe, production specialist

Photo Credits
Shutterstock: 3445128471, 21, Africa Studio, cover, 20, Andrea Izzotti, 11, Andrey_Kuzmin,
cover, bookzaa, 14, Boris Ryaposov, 6, DmitriMaruta, 19, gameanna, 22-23, Jonutis, back cover,
1, Kekyalyaynen, cover, maggee, 16, MEMEME, 10, Muh, 18, NorGal, 15, Oleinik Dmitri, 12,
pupunkkop, 13, Riccardo Mayer, 5, saknakorn, 17, science photo, 3, 9, tammykayphoto, 8,
trekandshoot, 7

Note to Parents and Teachers

The Here to There set supports national curriculum standards for science and social studies
related to technology and the roles of community workers. This book describes and illustrates
the journey water takes from water treatment plants to homes. The images support early
readers in understanding the text. The repetition of words and phrases helps early readers in
understanding the text. This book also introduces early readers to subject-specific vocabulary
words, which are defined in the Glossary section. Early readers may need assistance to read
some words and to use the Table of Contents, Glossary, Read More, Internet Sites, Critical
Thinking Using the Common Core, and Index sections of the book.

Printed in China.
007502WAIMS16

TABLE OF CONTENTS

Where Water Comes From

We need water every day

for drinking, washing, and cooking.

We even use it in our toilets.

Do you ever wonder how it gets there?

Water comes from lakes,
rivers, and underground.
Water treatment plants clean it.
Filters remove fish, plants, and
dirt from the water.

Water treatment plant workers
make the water safe to drink.
They add chemicals to the water
to kill bacteria.

How Water Moves

Treated water is pumped

into large water towers.

Water towers store the water

until people need it.

Water moves from water towers

to buildings through pipes.

The pipes are buried underground.

They may be made of metal

or plastic.

Water at Home

Plumbers install and fix pipes, sinks, and toilets in buildings. They use tools such as wrenches and pliers.

Some indoor pipes connect
to faucets. Other pipes connect
to toilets. When you flush,
waste goes down a drain.

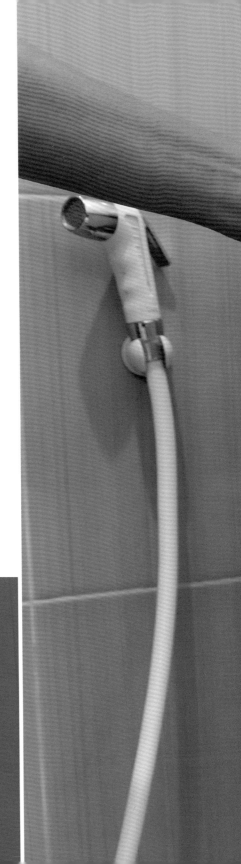

Dirty water moves through pipes from buildings to wastewater treatment plants. These plants clean the water. Then they send it back to lakes and rivers.

Saving Water

You can do your part
to save water. Run the dishwasher
only when it is full. Turn off
the faucet while brushing your teeth.
Take shorter showers.

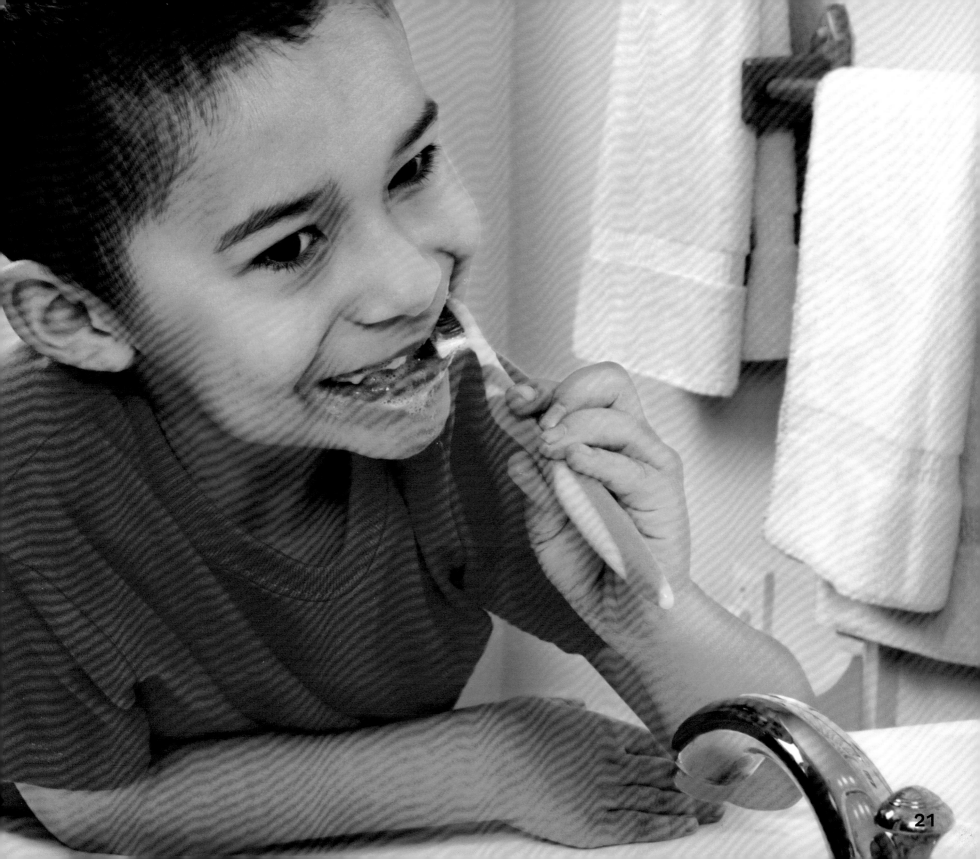

GLOSSARY

bacteria—very small living things that exist all around you and inside you; some bacteria cause disease

chemical—a substance used in or made by chemistry; many different kinds of chemicals can be used to clean water

faucet—an object with a valve that is used to control the flow of water; people use faucets to turn water on and off

filter—a device that cleans liquids or gases as they pass through it

install—to put in and connect for use

plumber—someone who puts in and fixes pipes, sinks, toilets, showers, and bathtubs

wastewater treatment plant—a place where water is cleaned before it is sent back to lakes and rivers

water treatment plant—a place where water is cleaned and stored before it is sent to homes and businesses

wrench—a tool used for tightening and loosening bolts and nuts

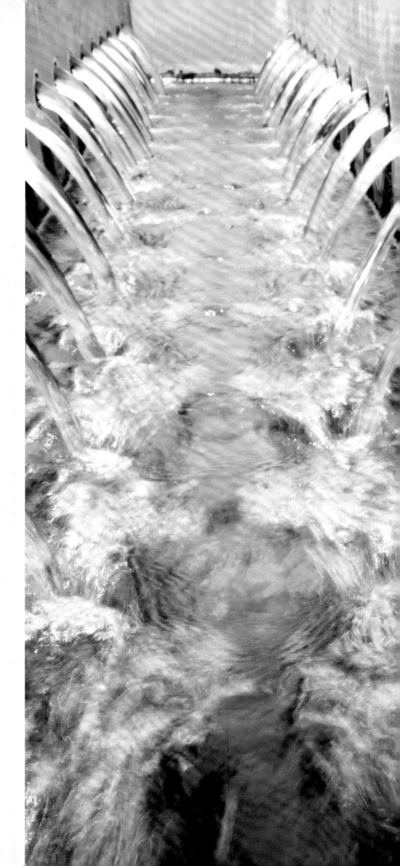

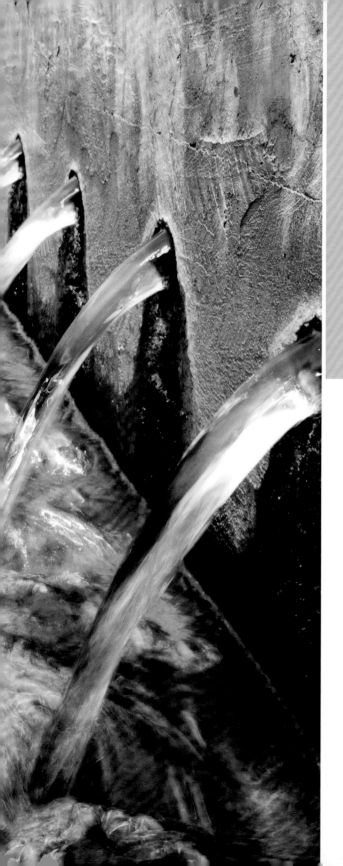

READ MORE

Hammersmith, Craig. *The Water Cycle*. Earth and Space Science. Mankato, Minn.: Capstone Press, 2012.

Meister, Cari. *Plumbers*. Community Helpers. Minneapolis: Bullfrog Books, 2015.

Rustad, Martha E. H. *Water*. Smithsonian Little Explorers. North Mankato, Minn.: Capstone Press, 2014.

INTERNET SITES

FactHound offers a safe, fun way to find Internet sites related to this book. All of the sites on FactHound have been researched by our staff.

Here's all you do:

Visit *www.facthound.com*

Type in this code: 9781491484357

Super-cool stuff! Check out projects, games and lots more at
www.capstonekids.com

CRITICAL THINKING USING THE COMMON CORE

1. Describe what happens to water at a water treatment plant. (Key Ideas and Details)

2. Explain why plumbers are important. What might happen if there were no plumbers? (Integration of Knowledge and Ideas)

3. Name two things you can do to save water. (Key Ideas and Details)

INDEX